How to
Write & Publish
Your Inspirational
Short Story

By Kristen Clark
Lawrence J. Clark, PhD

KRISTEN CLARK and LAWRENCE J. CLARK, PhD

American Mutt Press

ISBN-13: 978-0976459156
ISBN-10: 0976459159

DEDICATION

We dedicate this book to every writer - young and old, new and established – who has a heart for sharing their experience, strength, and hope with others. We pray for your ability to press on in your effort to share the very personal and powerful message God has given you. You have a message. The world needs to hear it.

Visit us online and find many more useful resources at:
http://TheCommunicationLeader.com/inspirationalwritingresources

CONTENTS

WHY COMPILATION BOOKS

MARKETING & MONETIZING YOUR INSPIRATIONAL SHORT STORY

INSPIRATIONAL SHORT STORIES FOR YOUR READING PLEASURE

Visit us online and find many more useful resources at:
http://TheCommunicationLeader.com/inspirationalwritingresources

KRISTEN CLARK and LAWRENCE J. CLARK, PhD

HOW WE GOT STARTED

KRISTEN CLARK and LAWRENCE J. CLARK, PhD

THE TURNING POINT IN MY WRITING ADVENTURE

Kristen Clark

Any man who keeps working is not a failure.
He may not be a great writer, but if he applies the
old-fashioned virtues of hard, constant labor, he'll
eventually make some kind of career for himself as writer.

Ray Bradbury

As a professional speaker, I understood the role writing played in my marketing strategy and began putting pen to paper a number of years ago in an effort to build my platform (a publishing business term that means a loyal base of fans who are potentials buyers of your book). Professional speaking is my first love and real talent. It is in this area I excel and it's one of the activities I love most. Unfortunately, my experience as a writer began less successfully.

At the advice of a colleague, I started out writing "how to" Ezine articles to build my credibility and expand my reach, but I found the process too formulaic for my taste. I wanted my writing to flow naturally but I was distracted by keywords, resource boxes, anchor text, and having enough affiliate links to make the submission worth my while. I wanted more freedom to express myself than I found allowable through this vehicle, and since my writing felt forced, I lost interest.

It was also suggested that I write a book, but I wasn't quite sure I had the patience or focus for a project of that magnitude. While I felt more comfortable using my natural writing style, the stress of creating hundreds of pages of real content was overwhelming and the practice of submitting query letters and book proposals was painful. This route was equally daunting and dissatisfying.

I submitted works for magazines, association newsletters, and various trade journals, and although I had some success with publications, writing had become more of a chore than the spiritual delight I heard others speak about.

I also felt defeated because the business of writing as part of my marketing mix just wasn't panning out. As a result, my confidence as a speaker also started to deteriorate. After all, I had heard on more than one occasion that speaking and writing fit together like a hand and a glove.

"Why don't you think about writing inspirational stories for compilation books?" a friend proposed. "You might enjoy that kind of writing and you could write about the same experiences you speak about."

That suggestion resonated deeply in me. I liked the potentially larger audience reach compilation books could create, and the thought of writing about my own personal life lessons was extremely appealing.

I took the time to investigate opportunities and discovered a number of publishers in search of well-written inspirational stories. Finding the publishers was fairly easy, thanks to the Internet, and it didn't take long to identify a few projects nicely suited for my areas of interest. I looked them over, narrowed the choices to one, and sat down to write.

Surprisingly, writing my first inspirational story was everything I dreamt writing could be. I felt newly inspired to share my experience, strength, and hope for the purpose of encouraging others, and I wrote with more passion and intention than ever before. My personal message flowed easily from my heart to the paper, and I knew immediately that this kind of writing was something I could actually do well. I wrote and wrote, and I submitted to dozens of publishers.

As you can imagine, butterflies of excitement soared through my body when I read my first story in a compilation book; I was so proud and felt validated and encouraged.

That day marked the turning point in my writing adventure, and I now consider myself a professional speaker *and* published author. After having published numerous print and online articles, blog posts, inspirational short stories, and even an award winning book, writing is no longer a chore. It remains a key ingredient in my overall marketing strategy and a primary vehicle for my message.

I hope this book will encourage and enable you to begin (or continue) your own journey of writing inspirational short stories; writing in this genre has given me a "new lease" on my (writing) life, and it is my hope and prayer that it will do the same for you.

MY LIFE-LONG LOVE AFFAIR WITH WRITING

Lawrence J. Clark, PhD

"When you catch an adjective, kill it. No, I don't mean utterly, but kill most of them – then the rest will be valuable. They weaken when they are close together. They give strength when they are wide apart. An adjective habit, or a wordy, diffuse, flowery habit, once fastened upon a person, is as hard to get rid of as any other vice."

Mark Twain

Unlike Kristen, my writing journey began at a very young age. I actually have a copy of a story I wrote when I was in second grade, about a group of explorers who come upon an old, dark castle full of bats and have to kill them all to save a princess. My mom typed it up at the time and recently gave me the original folded, creased, yellowed paper, dated October 28, 1968. Judging from the date, we can probably guess what inspired my interest in old castles and bats!

The following year I wrote an original play script, something about vampires and detectives, and we performed it for our school. Unfortunately I don't have the original script of that one, but the plot was probably plagiarized from some late-night black and white vampire movie combined with Sherlock Holmes or some other popular detective book or television show. I can't imagine anything very original coming out of the mind of an 8 year-old, but who knows?

Although I continued acting in school plays and writing occasional journal entries - I still have a small notebook in which I recounted our family's entire summer vacation camping out in the Appalachians and the beaches of Delaware and the Carolinas, including a very graphic description of my little brother throwing up in the back seat of our station wagon - writing creatively took a back seat for the next few years as I spent more time playing sports, doing activities with the Boy Scouts, and delivering newspapers for extra spending money.

It wasn't until my junior year of high school that I took a short story writing class from Mrs. Phoebe Eisenberg, who was diminutive in stature but an intellectual giant, and a genius at helping troubled young teens like me find an avenue to safely display our emotions through creating our own little worlds on the written page. Her class was one of the few in which I felt like what I said mattered, and her encouraging nature caused me to actually want to go to class - and pay attention - and participate in the discussions - and do the written exercises and homework.

A few weeks into the semester, I found myself laid up in a hospital for three days and then lying in bed for another week due to a sports injury and subsequent operation. Since I couldn't go to school or work, I turned to writing, again in the fantasy realm, and occupied my time creating my own little world. And when I say little, I mean very, very tiny. Well, the story wasn't tiny, but the subject matter was, as you'll soon find out . . .

I wrote what turned out to be a 27 page short story about a journalist who is sent to investigate strange happenings at the home and laboratory of an eccentric scientist. The journalist ends up being shrunk by the evil scientist's special Human Being Shrinker Gizmo, then placed into a terrarium lit only by a hazy, green glow coming through an emerald hanging from the top.

Inside the terrarium, he finds an assortment of odd characters who the scientist had previously shrunk, including, of course, a beautiful princess, with whom he gets to fall in love, save, and escape at the end of the story. I had unwittingly written what I now teach university students is a common motif in literature - the flawed hero's journey to battle against an evil protagonist and encounter various obstacles along the way before the climax of the story, in which he achieves his goal of finding the buried treasure, or saving his tribe or country or the entire world, or in this case, getting the girl and helping the rest of the shrunken captives escape and unshrink them-selves.

These first few experiences with writing, though nothing extraordinary or worthy of literary acclaim, made me realize that I was born with a gift, and that is to create characters and situations, or in the case of inspirational short stories, to take my own life experiences, and communicate them to others in a way that is entertaining, instructive, inspiration, or motivational. I am extremely grateful for this gift, and for the privilege to share my stories (and songs and plays and non-fiction books as well) with thousands of readers so far. And the inspirational short story is one of my favorite forms of writing, as it leaves the reader with a sense of hope and encouragement.

It is my hope that the words Kristen and I have shared in this brief volume will help you on your own writing journey, whether like me, you've been aware of your gift for many years, or like

Kristen, who discovered her gift later in life. Remember, this is YOUR journey, and it will be what you make of it. Do it for the love of the written word. Do it for the joy of sharing and inspiring others. Do it to honor your Creator who endowed you with this gift. But DO it. Write, let it flow, and share it with others; you will be amazed at what will transpire.

KRISTEN CLARK and LAWRENCE J. CLARK, PhD

A FANTASTIC EXPERIENCE

"Don't worry about failures, worry about the chances you miss when you don't even try."

Jack Canfield, Chicken Soup for the Soul

I (Kristen) spend a lot of time in this book talking about my experience writing for *Chicken Soup for the Soul*, so I felt I should offer this simple disclaimer: I am not a *Chicken Soup for the Soul* representative or employee, and will receive no compensation from them for having written this book.

I am, however, an author who enjoys doing business with this company. As the longest standing publisher of compilation books, they treat their contributors well, and the benefits of doing business with them have far exceeded my expectations.

Just in case you are not familiar with the *Chicken Soup for the Soul* book series, here are a few facts you should know:

- The *Chicken Soup for the Soul* book series of over 250 titles has sold more than 110 million copies in the U.S. and Canada.

- *Chicken Soup for the Soul* books have been translated into 43 languages, published in over 100 countries, and have sold over 500 million copies worldwide.

- Retail sales of *Chicken Soup for the Soul*-branded products exceed $100 million per year in the U.S. and Canada.

- Total worldwide retail sales of *Chicken Soup for the Soul*-branded products have exceeded $2 billion.

- *Chicken Soup for the Soul* is one of the world's best-known brands; in the U.S., according to a Harris Poll, 88.7% of the public recognizes *Chicken Soup for the Soul*.

- *Chicken Soup for the Soul* receives an average of 100 stories per day.

Chicken Soup for the Soul publishes stories that appeal to a wide audience. They do not publish sermons, essays, or eulogies. They do not publish term papers, letters, or journal entries. They do not publish stories that are political or controversial in nature. They also do not publish biographical or testimonial pieces.

They simply publish exceptional and inspiring stories.

As a contributor, I enjoy the recognition that comes with having my stories published in a number of their books. I also enjoy access to their monthly newsletter, receive call for submission emails for upcoming books, and participate in luncheons hosted by the publisher for local contributing authors. All of this gives me a behind-the-scenes insight into the publishing world. It's been a fantastic experience!

Chicken Soup for the Soul also aligns well with my personal areas of interest. I like writing non-fiction and I love writing inspirational stories for the market they reach.

If you are interested in writing inspirational short stories for publication, I suggest you consider submitting for *Chicken Soup for the Soul.* They pay for stories, provide free copies of books to contributing authors, and make additional copies available for sale at discounted prices.

They are also an extremely prestigious writing credit to list on your resume. Publishers and authors everywhere know that story contributors to *Chicken Soup for the Soul* are "cream of the crop" writers and are taken seriously as authors.

KRISTEN CLARK and LAWRENCE J. CLARK, PhD

WRITING TIPS

KRISTEN CLARK and LAWRENCE J. CLARK, PhD

HOW TO WRITE AN INSPIRING SHORT STORY

A short story must have a single mood and every sentence must build towards it.

Edgar Allen Poe

William Faulkner once described short stories as the most demanding form of writing after poetry, to be followed by the less demanding art of novel writing.

True or not, if you're anything like us, writing inspirational short stories is extremely appealing. Each time we put pen to paper, we become newly inspired to write about our experience, strength, and hope for the purpose of encouraging others, and we write with deep passion and intention in the process. We hope you will enjoy the same experience.

Typical Features of a Short Story

Before we go any further, it might be a good idea to define what a short story is. Having their roots in oral story-telling traditions, short stories are typically written in the first or third person, and can be fictional or non-fictional works. They run (roughly) five to twenty pages in length, typed and double spaced, and focus on a specific lesson or significant event.

Short stories usually have one main character, maybe two, and the character is well developed, dynamic, and evolves (changes, grows, or learns some important life lesson) throughout the story.

Short stories have a beginning, a middle (or body), and an end that often closes with a punch. In the "inspirational" genre, the ending is often something the reader can take away and use, muse upon, feel good about, or feel encouraged by.

What makes them inspirational is that they are written with "heart" and contain an emotional element of hope and encouragement. They often convey a personal message or unique point of view, and help readers see their lives more clearly in an effort to better understand their own personal experiences.

Great writers understand the basic storytelling elements and begin by identifying five primary components:

1. **The protagonist:** the character that drives the storyline. This may be you in a non-fiction story written in the first person, or a fictional character in a story written in the third person. Either way, this is the main character.

2. **The setting:** the story stage. This is where and when the story takes place.

3. **The conflict:** the obstacle that results in the lesson or significant experience of your main character. The obstacle can be people, places, or events. It is the problem that needs a solution.

4. **The climax:** the breaking point or peak of the story. This is the release your main character finds after a long and arduous struggle against some obstacle. The obstacle could be another character, but could also be the weather, a tragic event, or a change in circumstances, such as death or divorce. In some cases, the obstacle may even be an emotional or spiritual hurdle that is overcome by the main character.

5. **The resolution:** the solution or outcome. In the case of inspirational short stories, the outcome is usually encouraging, cheerful, and uplifting. Although not all solutions need to be happy, they can be equally effective if they are simply appropriate and leave open the possibility of a happier ending down the road.

Take the time to identify these five components for your story <u>before</u> you start writing. This can be done on paper or in your head.

I (Kristen) like to start my stories with an outline so I can mentally flush out these elements before I begin crafting my storyline.

Also, an outline helps me focus on the story thread, keeping me from rambling all over the place and making it difficult for my reader to follow along.

I (Lawrence) rarely create outlines when writing short stories. Instead, I may start with a memory of a specific incident or main point in mind, then will do a "brain dump" on paper and see where it takes me. This often leads to many unnecessary words being written, but then I go through and tighten it up by eliminating non-relevant dialogue or description, or use Mark Twain's method of "killing off" as many adjectives as possible.

Which method is correct? Answer: the one that works best for you! The key here is that a short story focuses on one incident, meaning it has a single plot, a single setting, a small number of characters, and it covers a short period of time. This is what makes it "short."

THE ART OF GETTING STARTED

Fill your paper with the breathings of your heart.

William Wordsworth

If you're new to writing short stories, you might find the task of getting started a little challenging. In fact, when asked what was the most frightening thing he had ever encountered, novelist Ernest Hemingway said, "A blank sheet of paper."

Where does one begin?

Follow these helpful suggestions and you'll be well on your way.

- Collect story ideas in a journal or notepad. These ideas can come from a variety of sources, including newspaper and magazine articles, radio or television programs, a conversation overheard in line at the grocery store or on a bus or airplane. Jot them down as quickly as you can after they come to you.

- Learn how to brainstorm and look to family and friends for inspiration and possible story lines. Of course you'll want to change names, dates, and places, to protect the guilty and preserve relationships. In fact, although they are an excellent source of material, be wary of using family and friends, especially if you are portraying any of them in a negative light.

- Remove all distractions and just focus on writing.

- Choose a topic that holds your interest.

- Begin with the basics, and outline your thoughts (again, on paper or just in your head) about the:

    1. introduction
    2. initiating action
    3. action leading up to the climax
    4. climax
    5. conclusion
    6. resolution

- Know your characters and note their personalities, quirks, favorite sayings or slang terms, and roles in your story. We'll discuss more about characterization later.

- Identify the one main event or sequence of a few events that occur in a relatively short period; this will become the "framework" of your story. It will also help you avoid giving too much background information.

- Decide the viewpoint of the storyteller (first, second, or third-person).

- Start writing!

A quick start is especially important in short stories because you don't have much room to elaborate on the details. Don't waste time on long introductions or descriptions of scenery, or fully developed characters complete with every detail of their lives; save that depth of writing for your next novel.

Instead, get right into the plot and get the story moving quickly in terms of action and dialogue. In literary terms, this is called "in medias res," which is Latin for "in the midst of things" (more about this later). Then let the story flow.

My (Kristen's) most successful inspirational short stories start out much this way. I start with an outline of ideas and then I write. I don't edit. I just write. I write until there's nothing left.

Then, I take a break, come back, and re-write. I tweak. I add. I delete. I move things around. I clarify. I embellish. I fill in with detail.

Then I take a break, come back, and re-write again. I do this until I feel the story has reached the point where I can edit, proof, and polish the work.

I (Lawrence) prefer to skip the outline and begin writing rather quickly once the inspiration has hit me and I have a general idea of what I'll be writing. I often pump out the entire story in one sitting, then come back to it later for the editing process, which due to my training in literature and job as a university professor, is the "easy" part.

Again, neither method is right or wrong, and if you ask a room full of twelve writers how they approach writing a story, they'll probably give you twelve different answers.

The good news is the writing process doesn't have to be strenuous or stressful, and if you get started using the tips outlined in this chapter, you'll quickly find your story flowing freely and developing for your second, third, and fourth draft.

And after that you'll be ready for your second story, then your third, then your fourth, and each time the process will become easier and will flow more naturally as you find the methods that work best for YOU. The key here is to start the writing process and let the story write itself.

KRISTEN CLARK and LAWRENCE J. CLARK, PhD

THE POWERFUL OPENING

Words are a lens to focus one's mind.

Ayn Rand

Unless your audience is a captive audience, such as college students required to read a short story for a school assignment, most readers will decide if a story is worth their time and energy within the first few sentences or paragraphs. As a result, the opening needs to grab the reader's attention quickly.

As mentioned earlier, one way to write a powerful opening is to use "in medias res," which is a literary technique that involves beginning your story "in the middle of things" and plunging into the heart of the action, drama, or conflict.

For example, let's say the event that kicks off your story involves a middle-aged woman being left at the altar on her wedding day. Your story will be less interesting if you start with the woman rolling out of bed that day and heading downstairs for breakfast, recounting every uneventful and less than interesting step that brings her to the altar.

A more effective way to start the story is to begin in the middle of the ceremony, right at the time she discovers she has been abandoned. It might read something like:

> "Then came the first of what would become an endless stream of tears. Her mind swirled. She tried to stave off that old stinkin' thinkin' that told her this was her fault. How would she face the two hundred wedding guests sitting behind her?"

The story would then continue from there, but you've now accomplished your first and most important goal; you've captured the reader's attention. You can imagine the reader thinking, "Who is the woman? Why would she be left at the altar? What is stinkin' thinkin'? Why would she think it was her fault? Was it her fault? What will happen next?"

This is a common technique used in writing novels, and works equally well in short stories. It leaves the reader wanting more.

A second way to write a powerful opening is to open the story with dialogue. Writing dialogue doesn't have to be intimidating, and not much dialogue is needed for a short story to be compelling, but a story without dialogue is, well, probably an essay rather than a story.

In using dialogue, you want your characters to speak directly and you want the dialogue to sound natural. This is one reason why it's important to know as much about your characters as possible. You want write the dialogue just as they would speak and include any slang, technical jargon, regional dialect, or even incorrect grammar they would actually use.

When writing dialogue, make sure to use quotation marks correctly. You may consider including adjectives that describe what the character is doing while speaking, but be careful not to overuse them, as this is a sure sign of an amateur author. Is the character yelling, whispering, laughing, or running out the back door? Use an adjective to describe this if it helps set the scene and is not obvious, otherwise, take Mark Twain's advice and "kill it off."

This is a great opening from a short story called "Loopy Love", written By Kara Johnson and published in *Chicken Soup for the Soul: Married Life*. It starts out like this:

> "And then, they took me into the intimidation room where they... they pulled out this big scary machine and started to torture me," he said as his eyelids drooped slowly again. I held his hand and brushed my fingers gently over his forehead and back into his hair.

Did that catch your attention? You probably can't wait to find out what the intimidation room is, why someone is torturing him with a big scary machine, and how he got there in the first place. This is a great example of opening with dialogue.

Another more colorful example can be found in the book, *Women in High Definition: Boldly Living Your Purposes with Vibrant Clarity*, written by Diane Markins. In her short story called, "Dying to Eat," she opens with:

> "Wanna see something cool?" Jan's older sister asked after they'd wolfed down a full package of cookies and were feeling pretty awful. She put her finger in her mouth, as Jan watched, and began to...

This opening is very descriptive (which is why I left the rest of the sentence off) but a great opening that starts with dialogue and uses the "in medias res" technique.

One way to ensure a powerful opening is to use what we call the "Sniff Test." One of our favorite sniff tests for a good story includes two simple questions: Do I care about the characters? Do I want to see what happens next?

In fact, we also use this sniff test when we're watching movies together or reading out loud together (which we do from time to time). We'll stop in the first ten minutes and ask each other, "do we care about the characters and do we want to see what happens next?"

Sometimes the answer is, "No, not really. This story just isn't doing it for me."

And then we move on to something else. We change the channel and look for another movie, or we close the book and select another. It's a great tool, and we use this same sniff test to evaluate our own writing.

You can use this simple method, too. Ask a friend or loved one to read the opening of your short story (just the first 2-3 paragraphs) and ask

KRISTEN CLARK and LAWRENCE J. CLARK, PhD

him or her these two questions:

- Do you care about the characters?
- Do you want to see what happens next?

The answers will tell you if you're opening is working or not.

THE COMPELLING ENDING

Great is the art of beginning,
but greater is the art of ending.

Henry Wadsworth Longfellow

Endings carry tremendous weight with readers. If they don't like the ending, chances are they won't like the short story. Worse, they won't like the author. Also, if the events in the story line are not satisfied by the ending, or the ending is not told well, the story will often be deemed poorly written.

And remember, inspirational short stories, unlike the often bleak and dismal short stories you may have been subjected to in your high school or college English class, need to end on an "up tone" and leave the reader with a feeling of encouragement or hope.

One of the problems faced by beginning short story writers is to decide when and how to end. One way to solve this problem ahead of time is to use Kristen's method of creating a story outline before you even start.

Another method, for those of us who prefer not to create a written outline, is to start with the end in mind, then work up to it. For example, if your main character is going to discover that forgiveness is a better state of being than bitterness and resentment, what is the "last straw" or final event that is going to help your character reach that conclusion?

There are, of course, many ways to do this. Here are a few types of endings you can choose from when writing your inspirational short story.

- **The barely there ending** is extremely brief and somewhat inconclusive. It alludes to what might happen next, but leaves much open to interpretation.

- **The real-life ending** clearly indicates what will happen to the characters with the results or outcome being realistic, maybe even mundane.

- **The surprise ending** has a dramatic twist and an unexpected outcome; readers never see it coming.

- **The classic denouement** explains what happened to the characters after the major climax and wraps up any loose ends in the plot.

- **The cheesy easy ending** (we think this should be an official literary term, since it occurs so frequently, especially in stories written by less experienced writers) is illogical and unrealistic, and written when the author has run out of space and can't tie things up neatly.

Inspirational short stories are designed to offer encouragement and hope to those in need, and those in need are looking for realistic and plausible solutions.

They are also looking for the unexpected solution that results in a happy or cheerful ending, because they want to feel hopeful that even in the midst of their own sorrow or confusion or pain or difficult situation, there is still a possibility that everything will work out for the best.

Make it a practice to write a path to the solution that is clear and reasonable. Readers should walk away with a sense of confidence because the ending is believable, and not a feeling of disappointment because the ending was a stretch.

A special note for those writing faith-based stories: the practice of writing a plausible ending includes writing an ending that is consistent with a faith's theology or beliefs, meaning that the ending is consistent with what believers of that faith are taught to believe as truth.

For example, if the ending is plausible based on a reader's theology, then it is a realistic solution. If the ending is inconsistent with a reader's theology, it may come across as nonsensical; the reader will not be able to relate, which is why it's important to understand our audience when we write. We'll talk more about identifying your target readers and carefully reading submission guidelines later in this book.

STORY WRITING TIPS

Get it down. Take chances. It may be bad, but it's the only way you can do anything really good.

William Faulkner

Need help with writing your story? Have a look at these tips for writers and check out the suggested resources at the end of this book.

- Do it. Write. Don't procrastinate.

- Start small, and go for detail.

- Write every single day.

- Read as much and as often as you can.

- Immerse yourself in reading the style or genre of writing in which you hope to be published.

- Keep a journal or notebook handy and jot down all of your brilliant ideas.

- Observe and use objects around you for inspiration.

- Use a dictionary and thesaurus to expand your writing vocabulary.

- Be descriptive (but not overly descriptive) of the characters, action, and scenery.

- Invest in a few valuable resources, including those listed at the end of this book.

- Learn the rules of grammar and how to break them effectively.

- Proofread everything at least three times before submitting for publication.

- Join a writers' group so you can gain support and feedback from a writing community.

- Subscribe to writing journals and magazines.

- Join writers groups on social media, and subscribe to blogs about writing; participate, learn, share, and enjoy!

- Use writing exercises to improve your skills, strengthen your talent, and explore different genres, styles, and techniques.

- Create a space in your home especially for writing.

- Find the time or times of day in which you can focus and be the most creative, and use that time to write.

- If it's not coming, don't force it; get up, take a walk, do some chores, etc., then come back to it later.

- Remember, writing should not be painful, strenuous, or stressful — let it flow naturally.

- Research your topic and avoid factual errors.

- Write compelling yet realistic dialogue.

- Deliver an "aha" moment.

- Tug relentlessly on the reader's heart and mind.

- Ensure that the depth of meaning and/or emotion you would like to convey is felt and understood by the reader.

- Show details by painting pictures for your readers.

- Leave the reader thinking - perhaps with a surprise twist or thought at the end.

Writing well, and especially writing for publication, takes practice. It also takes continued learning, an investment in resources, and fellowship with other writers. To be successful, we must submerge ourselves into the writing culture and embrace our role as the messenger.

Finally, remember that you are not just writing

for the sake of putting words on a page. For those of us who are writing inspirational short stories, this is our calling. This is our passion. This is our reason to write.

KEEPING IT
SWEET AND SIMPLE

Not that the story need be long,
but it will take a long while to make it short.

Henry David Thoreau

As published authors, we have learned to keep our writing sweet and simple. The sweet part is all about writing from the heart and from personal experience. It includes:

- Life lessons that are encouraging, uplifting, revealing, touching, and meaningful

- Celebration of the human spirit

- Profound ideas or enlightening events

- Imagery that lingers for days, even weeks

- Emotion, the kind that makes 'em laugh or cry, sometimes both at the same time

A well written inspirational short story will grab a reader's attention and cause him or her to marvel because it is truly sweet.

The simple is the short story formula and focusing on a single event or incident. It includes:

- A single plot
- A single setting
- A small number of characters
- A short period of time
- A single message of hope and inspiration

In keeping it simple, the reader is allowed to mentally replay the story over and over and meditate on the details of the isolated lesson or significant point.

This is the secret to success in writing inspirational short stories for publication. Keep the story sweet and simple. This is what Hallmark cards are made of and the reason *Chicken Soup for the Soul* is so successful.

Sweet and simple is what keeps readers engaged. It's what makes fans loyal. It's also what sells.

THE ART OF
EDITING WELL

*So the writer who breeds more words than he needs, is
making a chore for the reader who reads.*

Dr. Seuss

Editing is the next most critical process to writing. It is what separates the unpublished from the published. It is taxing, belaboring, and tricky, and there are no short cuts in editing. It is an absolute MUST.

Follow these suggestions when you edit each and every story. You'll be glad you did.

- Ask someone else to read your story and provide honest feedback.

- Stick to "said" over other dialogue tags in your effort to show realistic emotions. If the reader can't figure out that your character spoke the lines "angrily" or "cheerfully," rewrite the dialogue to make it more clear.

- Remove adverbs as these slow down your story. Remember Mark Twain's advice about adjectives and apply them to adverbs as well, both in descriptions of action and in dialogue.

- Eliminate unnecessary words (did you get that point yet?).

- Read your story out loud to catch any flaws in the flow of your words.

- Take your time and read your draft slowly and carefully; you'll be surprised at the number of mistakes you'll find, or lines of dialogue or description that could be written more clearly or succinctly.

- Worry about word count after you have finished your edits, not before, but do stick to the required word count in the submission guidelines (more on this later).

- Double check your facts and research, especially if you are not an expert in the subject, time period, etc.

- Put your work aside for a few days before editing a second or third or final time.

- Look to see if you have used the same word too many times.

- Check your writing for proper grammar and spelling. If grammar and spelling are not your "thing," you can still be a great

- writer, but be sure to have someone who is good at editing help you fix those issues before submitting for publication.

- Check for missing information, logical story structure, and content flow.

- Use proper punctuation. As with incorrect spelling and grammar, poor punctuation can cause your story to be thrown into the circular file, no matter how good the plot or message is.

- Read through your work in a different format. Try changing the font to 18 pt. temporarily, or better yet, print it out and read it on paper rather than on your computer screen.

- Remove unnecessary commas.

- Remove 10% of your words, especially adverbs, adjectives, and prepositions.

- Replace "stuffy" or archaic words with simple or more commonly used words.

- Remove the unnecessary "that" wherever possible.

- Avoid using the word "thing."

- Avoid the words "very" and "really."

- Ditch the passive voice. Use active voice

unless purposely trying to be vague. Remember to always include "who did what, and to whom" (i.e. not "the chocolate was eaten," but "Mary ate the chocolate").

- Avoid repeating the same point several times. Avoid repeating the same point several times. Avoid repeating the same point several times.

- When in doubt, take a break.

Eventually, you will need to stop the editing process. If you find yourself removing commas only to add them back in, or rewriting the closing paragraph and then putting it back in its original format, then you're done editing. It's time to get your work submitted for publication.

You may always have a nagging sense that your piece could still be better; however, perfection is an unattainable target. Learn to settle for "good enough." You'll never get published if you let perfection interfere with the submission process.

Practice these steps each time you edit and your writing will naturally improve. When your writing improves, your publications will increase.

WHY
COMPILATION
BOOKS

KRISTEN CLARK and LAWRENCE J. CLARK, PhD

COMPILATION BOOK PROJECTS AND WHERE TO FIND THEM

Writing is its own reward.

Henry Miller

Compilation books (sometimes referred to as anthologies) are simply collections of works by various authors. They may include fiction stories, non-fiction stories, or poetry. They are diverse in terms of content and style, and they provide a great opportunity to get writing credits.

Thankfully, there are a number of compilation publishers and projects out there, and finding them is fairly easy. Here are a few suggestions to get you started.

- **Search for "compilation book and call for submission" in your favorite search engine** and look for opportunities that align with your area of interest.

- **Search Amazon.com for "compilation books."** The results will yield various books and publishers to research further and contact for future book projects.

- **Attend writing conferences that have a compilation book project for writing credit**. You can easily find a writing conference to attend by searching the Internet, and a book project may be included in the conference fee or available at an additional charge.

- **Network with other writers** through clubs and associations. Your writing colleagues often know about upcoming projects and are willing to share about them. That's one of the great things about our industry.

- **Consider submitting for *Chicken Soup for the Soul***, Kristen's personal favorite publishing opportunity. It's free to submit a story, and publication in one of their books is considered a prestigious writing credit.

One of my (Kristen's) earlier publications was the result of attending a writing conference sponsored by CLASSeminars, Inc. They host a writing conference once or twice a year, usually in New Mexico, and include in their conference activities an opportunity to submit a short story for publication in their compilation book project.

They also make available people well established in the field of writing and publishing to help whip your story in shape for publication. Lawrence has served several times as a mentor for budding writers at this conference.

Once the book is available (usually within a few weeks after the conference) you can order copies to sell to friends and family, at your book readings and signings, or if you also a public speaker, in the back of the room at your speaking events.

With the help of the CLASS experts, one of my stories reached tip top shape and was good enough to be included in their book project. That gave me a solid writing credit and something to be proud of.

Once I got that story published in their compilation book project, I had the bug! Since then I've been published in numerous projects, including various books in the *Chicken Soup for the Soul* series, as well as other smaller yet also notable publications.

Remember, "seek and ye shall find." If you're interested in getting an inspirational short story published, take time to look for a compilation book project to submit for. They are out there, and they're waiting for YOUR story!

THE BENEFITS OF GETTING PUBLISHED IN A COMPILATION BOOK

All good writing is swimming under water and holding your breath.

F. Scott Fitzgerald

There are many benefits of writing for compilation books, including the myriad of creative marketing opportunities. Just consider the following:

- Publication in a compilation book gives you a writing credit and an opportunity to write a press release and post your accomplishment on social media.

- Many publishers will include your byline (including website or blog link), and in some cases your photograph.

- Larger, more well-known publishers will pay for your story.

- Many publishers will send you free copies of the book and allow you to purchase additional copies at discounted rates for selling at speaking events or online.

- Many publishers have an online submission processes, making it easy to submit your story.

- As a contributing author, you can leverage the publisher's brand in your marketing materials.

- Every author published in a compilation book becomes your selling agent, because every author included in that book reaches a fan base you will not reach on your own. Some of those readers will then visit your website, read your blog, and hopefully purchase other books your work appears in.

At the time of this printing, *Chicken Soup for the Soul* pays on average $200 for published stories up to 1,200 words and provides ten free copies of the book to the author. They also allow contributors to purchase additional copies of the book at discounted rates – sometimes as much as 50% off.

Chicken Soup for the Soul also provides an electronic newsletter filled with helpful tips for writing, suggestions for hosting book signings, and information about book sales.

Plus, they welcome multiple submissions. As a contributing author you can submit to a number of their different book projects all at the same time.

The icing on the cake, however, is that *Chicken Soup for the Soul* will let us leverage their name for marketing purposes, and their brand goes a long way. I (Kristen) often receive speaking opportunities just because I am a *Chicken Soup for the Soul* story contributor.

At one particular speaking event, I was introduced by the hostess, who articulated beautifully the introduction I had written for her about myself. I was proud when she read out loud my ministries and other accomplishments. Unfortunately, the audience seemed less than thrilled with all of my hubbub.

However, when the hostess concluded the introduction with her excitement about my being a story contributor to *Chicken Soup for the Soul*, I received a very generous applause.

After the event was over, I personally thanked her for the amazing introduction and for remembering to call out that last little detail.

She laughed and said, "Well actually, that's the

reason you're here today. The committee thought that was most impressive."

That's yet another great example of the benefits of leveraging a publisher's brand.

THE DO's AND DON'Ts OF GETTING PUBLISHED IN COMPILATION BOOKS

Don't tell me the moon is shining;
show me the glint of light on broken glass.

Anton Chekhov

If you have decided that writing for publication in compilation books is for you, congratulations! To make sure your experience is fruitful and rewarding, follow these suggested do's and don'ts. These have worked for us personally over the years.

Do:

1. Take time to research various publishers and book projects.

2. Participate in those projects that best align with your passion and interest.

3. Focus on the short story formula.

4. Write stories that are truly inspirational.

5. Grab the reader's attention with believable characters and dialogue, conflict, action, and (interesting and relevant) details.

KRISTEN CLARK and LAWRENCE J. CLARK, PhD

6. Write, re-write, and edit, edit, edit.

7. Follow the publisher's submission guidelines e-x-a-c-t-l-y.

8. Be patient.

9. Respond immediately to any communication from the publisher.

10. Accept the publisher's suggested edits and DO NOT argue with them; remember, if your story is one of the few that makes it to this stage of the process, it will more than likely be published if you follow the publisher's editorial suggestions.

Don't:

1. Submit a story that doesn't fit the project's theme.

2. Submit a poorly written story.

3. Rely too heavily on the spell-check feature of your word processor.

4. Pester the publisher with questions about the submission guidelines or book progress.

5. Inquire about why your story wasn't accepted for publication.

6. Submit stories that have already been

published elsewhere (unless specifically mentioned as acceptable in the submission guidelines).

7. Ask to submit rewrites after you've submitted your story to the publisher.

8. Argue with the publisher about suggested edits or changes to your story (see above).

9. Take rejection personally.

10. Procrastinate about revising and resubmitting your work elsewhere.

Take time to understand how the publishing process works. Be patient.

With *Chicken Soup for the Soul,* for example, I (Kristen) can submit a story and go approximately six to eight months before I hear a word about it. During that time I just wait patiently; I don't pester the publishing agent.

Once I do hear back, I am notified if my story made the first round.

Another month or two will go by and I'll hear if my story made it to the final round.

Another month or two will go by and they'll send me the story and ask me to proof it, because they have made a few minor edits. The story will at this point have a page number assigned to it.

Once I respond with my edits or approval, I will receive a contract to sign and send back. At this point time is of the essence, and they want the signed contract returned within 48 hours.

In another month or so the book will be published and available for sale in stores.

That's when the real celebration begins!

BEWARE THE
REASONABLE EXCUSE

*He that is good for making excuses
is seldom good for anything else.*

Benjamin Franklin

An old Japanese Proverb suggests that fear is only as deep as the mind allows, and we believe there is a lot of truth in this. We believe we have control over how much fear we allow our minds to entertain.

Although this may seem off topic for a "how to" book about writing, it's an important thing to consider. As an author, how much fear do **you** allow your mind to entertain? What fear do you experience most?

- Fear of Inadequacy (being deficient, insufficient, or undersupplied; lacking in or being short in)

- Fear of Loss (loss of things, relationships, dreams, opportunities, life) or of not having enough (food, money, clothes, shelter)

- Fear of Failure (lacking in accomplishments, achievements, and success)

- Fear of Abandonment (being deserted, left behind, withdrawn or pulled away from)

- Fear of Hardship, Depression, or Devastation (being overwhelmed and helpless; experiencing suffering, pain, or difficulty)

Fear is dangerous because it provides a platform for our self-imposed justification. In other words, we make excuses, and excuses can have serious and lasting consequences; they can prevent us from ever reaching our full potential.

Here are the most popular excuses; unfortunately many of them seem "reasonable" at the time, so they are easy to justify. Do any of these sound familiar?

- I'm too busy.

- I don't have time.

- It's too late.

- I don't have the money.

- I don't know how.

- I don't know where to start.

- I'm not smart enough.

- I'm not an expert.

- My friends and family don't think I can.

- My friends and family don't think I should.

- I need to focus on the people who need me.

- I don't have anyone to do this with.

- I don't know the right people.

- It's not perfect yet.

- It's not my destiny.

- It's not God's plan.

- No one else is doing it.

- There aren't any guarantees.

Quick Tip: a reasonable excuse usually follows the word "because."

Reasonable excuses are also often just plain cop-outs. You've heard the phrase, "the devil made me do it." That's about as reasonable of an excuse as Eve's response to God in Genesis 3:13 about why she ate the apple, to which she replied, "The serpent deceived me, and I ate." Who actually made the choice and actually took the bite? The serpent? Hmmmmmm . . .

As an author, ask yourself:

- What excuses do I make most often?

- What am I settling for as a result of my excuses?

- Why am I making these excuses?

- How do these excuses prevent me from moving forward?

- How do they impede my ability to reach my goals as a writer?

Beware of reasonable excuses. Recognize them, investigate them, and overcome them. Avoid them at all cost. These "reasonable" excuses can single-handedly interfere with your ability to ever get published.

MARKETING & MONETIZING YOUR INSPIRATIONAL SHORT STORY

KRISTEN CLARK and LAWRENCE J. CLARK, PhD

WHERE TO PUBLISH YOUR INSPIRATIONAL SHORT STORY

*You don't write because you want to say something,
you write because you have something to say.*

F. Scott Fitzgerald

The next three chapters assume you already excel in the writing craft, know how to write inspirational short stories, and have a few finished works tucked away somewhere.

This section is also designed to help you explore ways to get the most mileage out of those inspirational short stories, and in terms of "mileage" we mean publication mileage, revenue mileage, and marketing mileage. So first, let's take some time to look specifically at publication mileage.

A critical question to ask yourself is "why am I writing inspirational short stories?" Your answer might be "to inspire and give hope to others," or may simply be, "to increase my writing credits." If that's you, then you will want to submit your works to as many publishers as possible. We recommend submitting to four vehicles:

The first vehicle is a compilation book publisher, such as *Chicken Soup for the Soul.*

Purchase a copy of the current *Writer's Market* and start looking for publishers who accept unsolicited submissions of short stories. Or do some research on the Internet. We often find out about great compilation projects by searching the Internet, or simply by paying attention in social media groups we belong to and email lists to which we subscribe. Also, network with fellow writers through associations and writing organizations.

Do your homework and identify the genres accepted, the preferred word count, and all of the other submission requirements. We recommend researching each publisher before sitting down to write a short story for one of its projects. That way you can write a story that is directly in line with their needs, thereby increasing your odds for publication. It can also save wasted effort, as you might find that certain projects might be open to submissions only to members of a certain gender or religious denomination.

In the ever increasing world of self-published authors, look for authors managing and self-publishing their own compilation books. A writing credit is a writing credit, so take every opportunity to get your story published, even if it isn't with one of the top publishers.

The second vehicle is a magazine or journal that features short stories.

General interest magazines often feature an inspirational short story in each issue. Women's magazines are a great resource for inspirational short stories. Airline magazines also feature fun and fascinating short stories. Have you ever read through *Spirit Magazine*, a Southwest Airline publication? They publish short stories in every issue. Also, consider writing for *Guidepost Magazine* for their "Mysterious Ways" feature.

Many faith ministries and organizations, such as Charles Stanley's *In Touch Ministries*, publish magazines that feature short stories. They publish a monthly magazine filled with encouragement. Review our previous comments, though, and make sure you qualify and are comfortable with the organization's mission and beliefs before you submit.

Check out various magazines. Most of them publish their submission guidelines right on their website, and many pay for printed stories.

After you have identified which magazines you

want to target with your inspirational short stories, you'll want to order several back issues of the publication and familiarize yourself with the kinds of stories they publish. Editors will turn down a story if it even remotely resembles one they have published in the recent past, regardless of how well-written or exciting the story may be.

The third vehicle is short story contests.

Award-winning stories go a long way in terms of publication credits and look great on a resume. And there are plenty of contests for both unpublished and published authors.

Again, look for writing resources (like *Writer's Market* and the Internet) in order to find various contests. *Writer's Digest*, for example, has several contests throughout the year, all of which are listed on their website. Also, you'll want to be selective about which contests you enter, because contests usually have a fee for submission.

If this sounds like a fun challenge, then we suggest writing to the contest sponsor and requesting the manuscripts from the previous year's winners. This will give you great insight into the quality of stories that win awards.

You'll need thick skin for this project. Contests

are very selective and the winning stories are stellar in style and content. Make sure you're open to accepting feedback and rejection and learning how to improve your writing in the process.

If you win a contest, you'll want to promote the award at every opportunity. Make sure to include the award on your website, marketing collateral, and even by using stickers that you can place on the cover of any books your story might get published in.

Your work will be published, so there's your publishing credit, and you could earn anywhere from one hundred to a few hundred or even thousand dollars in prize money!

Finally, a fourth vehicle for publication is self-published compilation books featuring your own collection of inspirational short stories, or a collection of short stories you are editing and compiling of other authors' works. Easy to use online publishing tools, like CreateSpace, make this option more of a reality than ever.

If you choose this vehicle, feel free to partner with other authors and publish a combined collection of inspirational short stories. This approach can help you build a collection of stories quickly in the event you don't have enough content of your own to fill a book. Also, partnering with other authors can help defray the publishing costs.

We have published a number of short stories in self-published compilation projects. As contributing authors, we usually receive at least one free book, and we are often invited to purchase additional copies at half price to help fund the overall expense.

Those publication credits are worth the investment, as we can make up the cost by offering the books for sale on our product tables at speaking events and writing workshops.

HOW TO MONETIZE YOUR INSPIRATIONAL SHORT STORY

*It's none of their business that you have to learn to write.
Let them think you were born that way.*

Ernest Hemingway

It's a hard cold reality that there is little money to be made writing inspirational short stories. Professional pay rates average four cents per word, so a short story might net you $250, and even that is rare. That's not big money.

However, there are creative ways to grow your revenue stream and put a few more dollars in your pocket by capitalizing on the time you have already invested in the writing process and taking advantage of a few creative and paying activities.

Here are a few activities that have worked for us.

Offer live readings of your published and unpublished stories to groups that have a budget for entertainment or educational programs. Such groups include retirement homes, college and high school writing programs, writing conferences, and local libraries. Many groups and businesses will pay a small fee for a live reading, and will often allow you to sell autographed copies of your compilation books or other published works at the event.

I (Kristen) once sent mailers to local retirement homes offering to perform a live reading of my published inspirational short stories. Within two weeks I received my first booking, and I have been doing this ever since.

The pay averages $100 per event and not all events warrant selling my products. However, I can be selective about where I go and how far I'm willing to travel. An hour of time spent sharing my stories with a group of residents right up the road is certainly worth making one hundred dollars, and that doesn't even take into account the warm fuzzies I feel when I see the seniors enjoying my stories.

And I get to read the works I have already invested my time in writing, so there's no extra preparation required on my part. I do, however, need to be good at reading out loud, so I make sure to practice reading them a few times before doing so in public.

Host book signings and sales of compilation books featuring your published stories at establishments that don't have a budget for live events. This includes coffee houses, smaller libraries, and even grocery or department stores.

Invite fellow authors to attend and host the event with you. They can help you promote the event and add to the attendance by inviting their own fan base.

During event lulls, you and your colleagues can talk and share ideas. Some of the best writing and marketing collaboration takes place at events like these.

One of the benefits of writing for compilation books is that many of the publishers make it a practice of listing bylines for the contributing authors, and most of the bylines include the location of where that author lives.

You can quickly scan through the list of contributing authors, find those in your area, contact them, and see if they would be willing to co-host an event in your local town or city. It's a great way to network, meet other writers, get your name out in the marketplace, and fill the room.

Add some sizzle to your event by hosting a contest or giveaway with the prize being a collection of donated books from each of the participating authors. Be creative.

One author friend held a contest at an event for a chance to be named as a character in the author's next book. What a great idea!

Teach workshops on writing inspirational short stories and include your own stories as examples of published works.

Local community colleges and continuing education programs are always looking for new and fresh courses to offer, and they pay contracted instructors a percentage of the student's tuition.

Writing conferences are another venue to grow your revenue stream. Make sure to partner with an organization or association that can afford to pay for your services, travel costs, and conference fees.

Another way to add to your return on investment is to record yourself reading your stories to sell at online and offline events.

This is a fairly easy process and requires a minimal investment in technology. At the very least, you can do this with a handheld digital recorder, audio editing software, and a CD drive and burner.

I (Kristen) often record my stories on a digital recorder which I purchased for approximately $75. Once the session is recorded and downloaded to my computer, I use Audacity software, a free sound editor and recording software, to remove the ah's and um's and polish it up. Trust me when I say I'm no technology guru; anyone can do this.

Once the file has been edited, meaning I have removed any recording mistakes and errors on my part, I save the file as an MP3. That MP3 file can then be burned to a CD for sale. I add a clever label to the CD with my name and contact information, and a catchy title that tells buyers what the CD contains, and I offer it for sale either online or at in-person events.

You'll be amazed at how many people still like to be read to, especially in the car while they are driving.

Try any one of these ideas in your effort to grow your revenue stream and repurpose your inspirational short story as much as possible. After all, you put a lot of hard work into writing it. Don't let all that hard work go to waste.

KRISTEN CLARK and LAWRENCE J. CLARK, PhD

HOW TO MARKET YOUR INSPIRATIONAL SHORT STORY

There is no greater agony than bearing an untold story inside you.

Maya Angelou

Michael Hyatt, author and former chairman and CEO of Thomas Nelson Publishers, says, "Writing a great book is half the job. The other half is embracing your role as the book's chief spokesperson. If you do this well, you have a chance of creating a long and successful writing career."

This is true of inspirational short stories as well. Writing them is half the battle. The other half is marketing your stories (and yourself as the author of those stories). Thankfully, this is easier to do than you might think.

Consider doing the following marketing activities in your effort to repurpose your inspirational short stories and increase the return on your writing investment.

- Publish excerpts from your inspirational

short stories on your website and blogs.

- Create video trailers featuring excerpts from your inspirational short story, with a link to the published story or compilation book.

- Create a recording (or several recordings) of yourself reading an excerpt from your inspirational short story to add to your website and blogs, and share the recording on your social media platforms.

- Create "photo-quotes" with quotations from your inspirational short story to share on your social media platforms.

- Include quotes from your inspirational short stories on your business cards, bookmarks, author bio, and other marketing collateral.

- Include excerpts from your inspirational short stories in author interviews.

- Include excerpts from your inspirational short stories in press releases.

- Create event posters featuring a quote from your inspirational short story.

- Offer a free inspirational short story to readers who sign up for your mailing list or opt in to your auto-responder (this is a software program that automatically sends messages to large groups of people who have previously bought your books, attended your live events, etc.) For more information on autoresponders and other online marketing tools, see our resource page.

- Create a series of gift items featuring quotes from your inspirational short stories, including calendars, greeting cards, coffee mugs, and t-shirts. You can do this for free on several websites, and order them in bulk or let readers order them one at a time. There are many online companies who are more than willing to create this items for you, so don't think you need to be a world-famous author before you try this idea out. In fact, if you have a catchy slogan or quote, the gift items can actually inspire people to purchase your book!

Chicken Soup for the Soul is the master at re-purposing content. They offer three free stories from their book series to subscribers each month. Readers can download the stories from their website, or have them emailed directly to their inbox.

The point here is to repurpose the content you've

already created and find ways to include that content in your marketing activities. Use quotes from your inspirational short stories to make a point, support a theme, and add interest. And, don't forget – a quote can simply be a piece of dialogue for added interest.

INSPIRATIONAL SHORT STORIES FOR YOUR READING PLEASURE

MAKING TIME TO READ

*If you don't have time to read, you don't have time
(or the tools) to write. Simple as that.*

Stephen King

We know it may seem odd to quote an author known more for ghastly tales about vampires, monsters, and other grisly subject matter in a book that is about writing uplifting and encouraging short stories, but we did so for two reasons. One is that you can find inspiration anywhere. The other is that Stephen King, whether you are a fan of his writing or not, has sold a gazillion books, and definitely knows what he's talking about when it comes to the craft of writing and the business of getting published.

The point is, we all know we should read more. We should read to learn the rules, understand the language better, and decide which stories work and which don't. But do we? As we have mentioned in previous chapters, it's essential to read stories, especially stories in the genre in which we'd like to be published.

Reading helps us appreciate the turn of a phrase,

the finer points of words, and ideas to expand upon. Reading helps us push past writing plateaus and roadblocks, and challenges us to improve our craft.

So ask yourself, "Do I read enough?," and "Am I reading the type of stories I would like to write?" "Am I making time to read as well as to write?"

Take an important step in becoming a good writer by reading the inspirational short stories provided in the next five chapters, then go read inspirational stories that have been published by the companies you would like to publish your next (or first) story.

We are confident that doing so will not only inspire your next writing session, but will encourage and uplift your spirit, which is, after all, the purpose of an inspirational short story.

Finally, we hope you enjoy our stories, and have discovered something useful in the preceding chapters. We invite you to visit our websites, join our social media groups, and share what you have learned and how you have applied it, especially how it has helped transform your approach to and practice of writing inspirational short stories.

THE CLOSE CALL WITH THE MAMMOGRAM TECHNICIAN

Kristen Clark

As published in *Women in High Def*,
Snowfall Press

Morning came sooner than Barbara had hoped; she had been dreading this day all week. Soon, she would endure something she considered worse than a root canal. Barbara was scheduled for her annual mammogram and she could no longer put it off. She crawled out of bed and, in anticipation of the usual mild pain that accompanies this awkward ritual, swallowed the recommended dose of ibuprofen. She then consulted her calendar to confirm the appointment. Scribbled in pencil was the time *8:30am,* along with the note "arrive 20 minutes early to fill out paperwork."

The commute to her appointment was easy enough, and after the paperwork was filled out and turned in Barbara sat in the waiting room. She thumbed through a magazine and watched snippets of the news on the wall-mounted TV. She mentally reviewed her schedule at the office and wondered if she had enough shredded cheese to make her husband's favorite Cheesy Enchiladas for dinner. She watched a few other women come and go while she sat there in her oh-so-attractive lab gown, and she waited. After what seemed like an hour, Barbara grew impatient and asked the x-ray technician about her appointment.

The technician checked her clipboard and reported loudly, "Well, you aren't scheduled until 9:30, and it's only 9:35 now. By our standards we're right on time. You're next."

Barbara remembered clearly that her appointment was for 8:30am. Her mind played back the conversation with the appointment desk and her instructions to come in early to fill out the required paperwork, and Barbara had done just that. Barbara asked the technician to double check her schedule.

The technician looked at her clipboard again and tapped her pen on the paper as she announced even more loudly, "It says right here that your appointment is for 9:30. You must have written it down wrong on your calendar. We don't make mistakes like that."

Barbara was insulted. She knew how to keep a calendar and manage a schedule. She was used to managing projects and timelines all day long at work, after which she would herd the family through dinner, homework, showers and night-nights. Barbara maintained a tight schedule just to keep her sanity, and she knew that her appointment was scheduled for 8:30am. She had made no mistake.

Barbara prepared to launch a verbal attack. She leaned forward on her toes, straightened her shoulders, looked the technician directly in the eye, and froze. In a split second Barbara realized that the technician would soon control the very device that would have an unrelenting grip on her prized body parts. Barbara asked herself, did she really want to give this woman a hard time? Was it going to be worth it?

A friend's favorite mantra floated through Barbara's mind, "What's more important? Do you want to be right? Or do you want to be happy?"

In this case being right seemed less important and being happy meant coming through the experience free from severe pain or bodily harm.

Barbara laughed to herself. She certainly didn't

want to make the situation more difficult. She relaxed and both feet fell flat on the floor. She drew a slow and calming breath and offered her most humble and sincere smile.

She replied, "You might be right. I apologize. I must have gotten the time wrong, which means then that we're right on schedule."

Fortunately, the encounter with the technician was short lived; Barbara was in and out in no time and with all of her body parts intact. In fact, Barbara managed to escape without even a wince, and as she later recounted her close call to her husband, they both laughed in agreement - sometimes it is better to be happy; being right is overrated.

GET ME OUTTA HEAH!

Lawrence J. Clark

As published in *Echoes of Mercy*,
WinePress Publishing

"Sometimes we disobey God out of arrogance," the conference speaker said, "and sometimes out of pride or fear." I began recounting the numerous situations in my life to which this applied.

"I'll never go back to a nursing home again," I proudly announced at dinner.

I was thirteen and looking for a way to earn spending money; in rural Southern Maine there weren't many options, but thankfully, my friend Timmy offered to sell me his paper route for twenty dollars, including one day of on the job training, so after school we walked from one end of town to the other so I could learn the route. One of the customers was the county nursing home, so Timmy introduced me to the staff.

"We get busy sometimes, so just leave it on the

nurse's station," a lady in a green hair net told me. Easy enough, I thought. The next day I strolled down the long hallway and dropped the paper on the desk. Just before I made it back to the front door, though, a wheelchair-bound patient grabbed me by the arm.

"You gotta get me outta heah!" she pleaded in a thick Maine accent. "You gotta call my kids; I'm bein' held hostage and they don't know I'm heah!"

I gulped a lungful of antiseptic air and stared down at her emaciated body; her sunken eyes stared up at me, pleading for assistance, so I did what any normal 13-yr. old boy would do— peeled her bony fingers off my arm, ran out the door, and never went back.

And when I say never, I mean never. Not to that nursing home or any other.

Later, while in college, I signed up for a summer missions program; they assigned me to a small church in Worcester, Massachusetts.

"Here are your duties for the summer," the program director explained. "Work with the youth group, play guitar on Sunday mornings, and conduct a prayer service on Wednesday nights."

"Ok, cool," I said, already thinking up fun games and activities for the kiddos.

"Oh yeah . . . I almost forgot. The assistant pastor is taking the summer off, and he leads weekly services in three area nursing homes. You can handle that, too, right?"

I wanted to heave. I wanted to go find a job waiting tables or washing dishes or picking blueberries--anything other than spend the next ten weeks cooped up in some smelly old folk's homes.

But then I remembered my promise to God at a revival service earlier that year. "I offer You myself, my gifts, and my talents. I will serve You, no matter what, no matter where, no matter how."

"Uh, sure," I muttered.

The first day wasn't easy; the antiseptic odor and gloomy atmosphere reminded of my earlier horrifying experience. Eventually, though, I got to know many of the residents and developed compassion for these once proud and hard-working, but now completely dependent people, who were destined to live the rest of their lives without ever leaving that building. Some were blessed with families who visited often, bringing books and treats from their favorite restaurants and bakeries, but some had no one, or at least no one who took the time to visit, give them a hug, and provide a break from their otherwise monotonous existence.

God honored my commitment by helping me overcome my fear of nursing homes and old people in general, and sparking my creativity. That summer I wrote a song, "Running Out of Time," that has touched many hearts and remains in my repertoire to this day. I later turned the song into a poem that I often read in schools and libraries.

In the past couple of years I have also performed in over a dozen nursing homes; one show was in Pittsfield, Massachusetts, at the same nursing home where my 92 yr. old grandmother was living. We took photos of her holding my poetry and short story book. She remembered the cover picture--my dad and me standing in front of our 1957 Ford. She told me how proud she was that her grandson was a published author, a dream that she had held when she was younger.

She passed away shortly afterward, so I was grateful for our final visit that God had prepared me for thirty years earlier. As I think about the times God has continually (and continues to) rescue me from my arrogance, pride, and fear, the echoes of his mercy grow louder and deeper.

KRISTEN CLARK and LAWRENCE J. CLARK, PhD

THE GRATITUDE LIST

Kristen Clark

As published in *Transformed: Renewed and Changed by the Power of God,*
WinePress Publishing

"Personally," she whispered, "I think the reason you have such a miserable life is because you have a bad attitude."

I could always count on Jennifer to tell me what I needed to hear whether I wanted to hear it or not. I had been complaining about my growing mound of bills while failing to celebrate a bonus I had received at work. She quickly realized my problem.

"What you need is an attitude adjustment. You need to develop an attitude of gratitude," she continued.

She was right. I was the Queen of Entitlement and Expectation and had mastered the art of judgment and criticism. I called bank tellers idiots when they asked for my account number the second time. I berated customer service representative for putting me on hold longer than five minutes. I accused the dry cleaning clerks of sheer stupidity when the spaghetti stain remained evident on my pale pink blouse. I dismissed good friends for not dropping everything to accommodate my needs, and then complained to anyone who would listen. On many days I was outright mean.

As a new Christian, I understood how developing thankfulness was God's will for me. I was undergoing a transformation, one that included developing the same mindset and attitudes as Christ, which meant being prayerful, joyful, and grateful in all circumstances. Unfortunately, I struggled with the part about being grateful.

Thankfully, I have always been motivated by pain and become willing to do something different when I am uncomfortable in a given situation. By this time, I was miserable. I had reached my all-time low – emotionally, physically, mentally, financially, and spiritually.

"Why don't you try keeping a gratitude list," my friend offered. "Write down three things each day that you are grateful for."

I took her suggestion to heart and began the

adventure of writing a daily gratitude list, only I wasn't very good at it. My initial lists were overly simplistic and uncreative or uninspiring.

The roof over my head.

The food in my pantry.

A steady paycheck.

These everyday items were the extend of my gratitude until Jennifer suggested I write down three things I am grateful for each day without listing the same thing twice – ever.

Ooh, that was tough! But the added caveat forced me to look more closely at the details of my life, including those things I had taken for granted over the years. The Bible tells us those who seek good will find good, and it didn't take long before I stared to understand just how blessed my life really was.

A few months later, I read Proverbs 15:15, which states, "For the poor, every day brings troubles; for the happy heart, life is a continual fest." That single verse resonated deeply in my spirit, and I quickly grabbed my Bible to see what else was written about gratitude and attitude. I was thrilled with what I found.

I read about how attitudes can shape personality and, while we cannot always choose our circumstances, we can choose our attitude about them and focus on things that are true, pure, and lovely.

Today I am grateful for Jennifer's honesty and willingness to suggest my attitude needed a transformation. With her help, and through daily prayer, I began a journey through which I now see God's numerous blessings in my life. Today, my gratitude list celebrate those blessings:

- The teller who asked for my account number the second time as a security measure.

- The representative's effort to solve my problem, no matter how long I waited on hold.

- The clerk's success in removing most of the evidence of my clumsiness with food.

- The grace my friends have shown me over the years and how valuable their friendship is.

Ah, life is good!

THE CHURCH OF OSCAR

Lawrence J. Clark

As published in *Transformed: Renewed and Changed by the Power of God,*
WinePress Publishing

"Two Big Smokies, extra onions on one, no mustard on the other . . . one Mrs. Smokie extra pickles!"

The cashier shouted her order in a thick southern accent that I could barely understand. Two weeks earlier I had moved to Knoxville, Tennessee on a whim.

I was 19 and single, and with my Choleric-Sanguine personality it sounded like a fun thing to do. And I was a hard worker, so I found a short-order cook job at the Smokey Mountain Market, where I met my new boss, Oscar.

"You need to get yourself a coat," he announced as I stood shivering in the damp, pre-dawn air. "Let's get you some coffee."

"Sounds good, eh," I said.

"New England?"

"Ayuh—Maine."

"Thought so--welcome to the real America, Yankee Boy."

His broad smile disarmed me, and Oscar soon taught me everything he knew; I learned to cook food I had never even eaten, like grits.

"Blech!!" I said, spitting them back out. "How can you eat this mush?"

"It's an acquired taste, Yank," Oscar laughed, slapping his thigh through his gravy-splotched apron.

One morning, while rolling out biscuit dough, my curiosity got the best of me.

"Oscar, how come you're working here? When I'm your age, I plan to be a millionaire living on my own island."

"Good question. I wasn't always a cook; I was once a bank president."

"C'mon . . ."

"I'm serious--worked my way through college--got promoted and married the day after graduation."

"Cool."

"Came from a mining family--I was the first to graduate college."

"Good for you—bank president, wow . . ."

"Working that hard is stressful, though--started drinking every night. I made life miserable for my wife and kids. Soon I was out of control, but somehow kept getting promoted."

"Cool."

"Maybe--I had the money, the company car, the country club . . ."

"I want all that!"

"Everything has a price, Yank. My wife and kids despised me. The bible tells us that the root of all evil is the love of money."

"You believe all that bible stuff?"

"Yes, sir--didn't always, though. I went to

Sunday school, but after college Christianity lost its relevance--just a way for politicians and corporations to keep ignorant folks dreaming about a better life in la-la land while they laughed all the way to the bank—my bank. I laughed, too, and treated the "little people" like peasants."

"I can't imagine that."

"Thanks, but I didn't change on my own. One night, after several cocktails, I had a severe heart attack and slammed into a tree. The Doc said I'd die within a year if I didn't quit my job--I realized power or money wouldn't do me any good six feet under."

"So what happened?"

"Drove straight to my boyhood church, sat for a long time, and thought about what a mess I was. I then tried to ask Jesus for forgiveness, but all I could do was cry. Afterward, though, a giant weight was suddenly lifted."

"I get that," I said, then told him about the time a year earlier when I was selling vacuums door to door. One night, after I finished my sales pitch, a guy got his bible and explained how everyone's a sinner, but God sent his Son to die so we could be free.

"But I don't see you going to church now, Yank," he observed. "And spending your time in clubs down on the strip isn't exactly the life Jesus wants for you."

"But that's where all my friends are, Oscar. You old guys can hang out in church, but that's not much fun for us."

"There are other ways to spend time with Him. I pray every morning at work--one of the things I love about this job. People leave me alone, for the most part."

"Except me, of course."

"Ah, you're alright, for a Yankee, anyway," he grinned. "Now enough of this chit-chat—we've only got fifteen minutes to finish these biscuits."

We shared many conversations after that, and Oscar taught me many lessons that I remember to this day. I started attending a young adult bible study, and a year later earned a scholarship to a Christian college where I continued my transformation into the likeness of Christ, a process that continues 30 years later. And I will never forget my very first church, the Church of Oscar.

KRISTEN CLARK and LAWRENCE J. CLARK, PhD

HE LISTENED

Kristen Clark

As published in
Chicken Soup for the Soul: Married Life

Christmas was three weeks away and my husband was fishing for ideas for my present. I smiled because he is always so thoughtful when it comes to buying Christmas gifts and I have never been disappointed by his choices.

"Actually," he announced, "I'd like to buy you some bras."

That got my attention and I listened intently as he explained that, while he was relatively familiar with the broader world of lingerie, he wasn't quite sure what size or kind of bra I would wear. He wanted some direction.

I paused. He waited. We sat together on the couch looking at each other with a funny smirk on our faces until I finally broke the silence.

KRISTEN CLARK and LAWRENCE J. CLARK, PhD

"I would love for you to buy me a bra, but what I really need are practical bras. I don't need fancy, frilly, romantic, lacy bras for our intimate rendezvous in the bedroom. I already have a wide variety of items for that, many of which you bought for me. What I really need are practical bras to wear during the day and your timing is great... mine are almost shot."

Disappointment spread across his face as I explained what I meant by practical bras. I needed at least three, all in neutral colors: one black, one white, and one ivory. I needed bras that were comfortable enough to wear all day long, and for me that meant bras with support but no underwire. I needed bras with a little padding so that I could avoid embarrassment while wearing a lightweight and formfitting blouse to the office during the summer months when the AC kicks into high gear. I needed bras that were solid color and sparing in lace and design because the additional detail, while pretty and feminine, might show through some of my more delicate, yet professional sweaters.

My husband paid close attention, but I could tell that practical wasn't what he had in mind. Regardless, I was delighted Christmas morning when I opened one of my many presents and found three practical bras: one white, one ivory, and one black! He had done it. My husband had listened carefully to my wishes and delivered on every aspect. I was so pleased I giggled with joy, and then he handed me my next present. Gently, I unwrapped three beautiful and sexy dresses, each one designed with lots of color, lace and fabulous detail.

"One to wear over each new bra," he said, and we both laughed out loud.

Those three bras turned out to be my favorite Christmas present and a fond memory. They were not overly expensive. They were not elegant or lavish. They were not even anything I'd want to brag about to our friends and family members. But, they were everything I asked for. They were also symbolic of my husband's effort to keep his wedding vows. On our wedding day, before God and many witnesses, we promised to be loving and faithful: in plenty and in want, in joy and in sorrow, in sickness and in health, as long we both shall live. Little did he know that "plenty and want" might someday include practical bras.

EXTRAS

SUGGESTED RESOURCES

NOTE: for an updated list and links to even more resources, please visit:

http://TheCommunicationLeader.com/inspirationalwritingresources

Writing Resources:

- *1,000 Creative Writing Prompts: Ideas for Blogs, Scripts, Stories and More* by Bryan Cohen

- *2014 Writer's Market* by Robert Lee Brewer

- *Crafting Novels & Short Stories: Everything You Need to Know to Write Great Fiction* by Editors of Writer's Digest

- *Elements of Style* by William Strunk Jr.

- *On Writing Well, 30th Anniversary Edition: The Classic Guide to Writing Nonfiction* by William Knowlton Zinsser

- *The Writing of the Short Story* by Lewis Worthington Smith

- *The Writer's Idea Book 10th Anniversary Edition: How to Develop Great Ideas for Fiction, Nonfiction, Poetry, and Screenplays* by Jack Heffron

- *Writing Tools: 50 Essential Strategies for Every Writer* by Roy Peter Clark

Technology Resources:

- Inexpensive digital voice recorder (we prefer the Olympus brand)

- Audacity audio editing software (Softworld.com)

- Website shopping cart and auto-responder (1ShoppingCart.com)

- PowerPoint for creating photo-quotes

- CreateSpace.com for creating self-published compilation books

NOTABLE PUBLICATIONS AND AWARDS BY THE AUTHORS

Becoming a Woman of Worth:
Creating a More Confident You
By Kristen Clark
Received the Gold Medal in
Christian Biblical Counseling
2014 Readers' Favorite Intl' Book Award Contest

- Platinum Expert Author status with Ezine Articles, Kristen Clark

- *How to Write & Publish Your Inspirational Short Story,* American Mutt Press, 2014, Kristen Clark and Lawrence J. Clark

- *Becoming a Woman of Worth: Creating a More Confident You,* American Mutt Press, 2014, Kristen Clark

- *30 Classic and Vintage Poems About Butterflies,* American Mutt Press, 2013, Kristen Clark

- "Get Me Outta Heah," *Echoes of Mercy,* WinePress Publishing, 2012, Lawrence J. Clark

- "He Listened," *Chicken Soup for the Soul: Married Life,* Chicken Soup for the Soul, 2012, Kristen Clark

- "Close Call with the Mammogram Technician," *Women in High Definition,* Snowfall Press, 2012, Kristen Clark

- "The Church of Oscar," *Transformed: Renewed and Changed by the Power of God,* WinePress Publishing, 2011, Lawrence J. Clark

- "The Gratitude List," *Transformed: Renewed and Changed by the Power of God,* Winepress Publishing, 2011, Kristen Clark

- "Jesus Freaks," *Out of the Overflow*, WinePress Publishing, 2011, Lawrence J. Clark

- "Never Alone," *Chicken Soup for the Soul: Christmas Magic*, Chicken Soup for the Soul, 2010, Kristen Clark

- "Hurricane Rita and Her Silver Lining," *Chicken Soup for the Soul: Count Your Blessings,* Chicken Soup for the Soul, 2009, Kristen Clark

- "The Pony-Tailed Guy Goes to School," *Moments of Grace*, Forever Books Publishing, 2008, Lawrence J. Clark

- *The Ballad of Dinkle and Other Kids' Favorites,* American Mutt Press, 2007, Lawrence J. Clark

- *The Magic of Mechanics*, American Mutt Press, 2006, Lawrence J. Clark

- "A Wretch Like Me," *Out of the Clueless Pit*, Windwood Presbyterian Church, 2005, Kristen Clark

Kristen continues to write inspirational short stories for publication with *Chicken Soup for the Soul.* As a member of the American Association of Christian Counselors, and frequent speaker on developing confidence as a spiritual mindset, she is also currently compiling a collection of heart-felt and provocative stories designed to speak powerfully to women in search of their value as Daughters of the King. When not writing, she shares her experience at writing conferences and seminars.

Lawrence has delivered hundreds of speeches, seminars, webinars, and live workshops in the past thirty years in a variety of venues, including businesses, civic groups, churches, libraries, public schools, universities, conventions and trade shows, community events, senior centers, and cruise ships.

He has also spent over twenty-five years teaching professional writing and communication courses, as well as creative writing and literature courses, at the university level, and supports the local community through his gifts and talents to help young people discover the value of reading and writing.

Additionally, he shares his personal story of dropping out of high school, then returning to eventually earn a doctorate, with at-risk-teens in an effort to show them that it's never too late to turn one's life around.

If you are interested in booking Lawrence or Kristen to deliver a workshop or keynote speech to your group, church, or conference, edit or critique your inspirational short story for publication, or provide group or personal coaching in writing, speaking, or the publishing business, please contact us at:

- Lawrence@thecommunicationleader.com
- Kristen@kristenclark.org

Visit us online and find many more useful resources at:
http://TheCommunicationLeader.com/inspirationalwritingresources

KRISTEN CLARK and LAWRENCE J. CLARK, PhD

www.ingramcontent.com/pod-product-compliance
Lightning Source LLC
Chambersburg PA
CBHW071556040426
42452CB00008B/1194